Foreword

The Royal Yacht *Britannia* was a proud and successful ambassador for Great Britain and the Commonwealth for over forty years. She dutifully served the Royal Family across the globe and played a key role in major historical events, including the handover of Hong Kong. It is little wonder that she still enjoys the enduring affection of the Royal Family, her former Officers and Yachtsmen, those who saw her sailing into ports around the world, and our own staff who now lovingly maintain her.

It is a great honour for Edinburgh's historic port of Leith to be her permanent home. As well as proving popular with visitors, *Britannia* is being well maintained and has experienced considerable success as a leading visitor attraction. On behalf of my fellow Trustees, I would like to record our appreciation of the great work and unstinting efforts of our dedicated staff - we are all proud to be serving *Britannia*.

Neil Rankin

Rear Admiral Neil Rankin CB CBE
Chairman of The Royal Yacht *Britannia* Trust

OFFICIAL SOUVENIR
GUIDEBOOK

Britannia in dry dock at Portsmouth, 1954

Contents

" I name this ship Britannia. *I wish success to her and to all who sail in her.* "

HM The Queen

The crowds cheer *Britannia* down the slipway as she is launched, 16 April 1953

> *Britannia is special for a number of reasons. Almost every previous sovereign has been responsible for building a church, a castle, a palace or just a house. The only comparable structure in the present reign is Britannia. As such she is a splendid example of contemporary British design and technology.*

HRH Prince Philip

The Building of *Britannia*

The Queen with Prince Philip at *Britannia's* launch

The Queen presides over the launching ceremony

The Queen's father, King George VI

When The Queen released a bottle of Empire wine against *Britannia's* bow, it was the first time that a reigning monarch had launched a Royal Yacht built for their own use.

Many coats of paint are applied to the hull

Clyde Built

On 4 February 1952, an Admiralty telegram instructed the Clydebank shipyard, John Brown & Co, to "proceed forthwith with detailed design and construction on fair and reasonable price basis of hull machinery of vessel referred to in your letter McN/MK dated 24th November". This order was confirmed in writing the next day. Sadly, King George VI, HM Queen Elizabeth II's father, for whom the ship was being built, died just one day later on 6 February 1952. It then became The Queen's responsibility to oversee the commissioning of the new Royal Yacht.

John Brown & Co was one of the most famous shipyards in the world with an impeccable pedigree, having been responsible for building the giant luxury liners *Queen Elizabeth* and *Queen Mary*. The building of *Britannia* began with the laying of the keel in June 1952.

Britannia was one of the last fully-riveted ships to be built. Her smooth-to-the-touch hull was achieved by the application of a special foundation layer and six coats of paint, and was a testament to the skills of John Brown's painters.

Just under a year after the hard work began, on 16 April 1953, the Royal Yacht was ready to be launched. The Yacht's name was a closely guarded secret right up until the last moment. On the day of the launch, The Queen revealed it to the waiting public with the words: "I name this ship *Britannia*. I wish success to her and to all who sail in her."

The Queen and Prince Philip arrive to launch *Britannia*

Sir Hugh Casson, the chosen designer for the Royal Apartments

A very personal touch

Britannia was not only the Royal Yacht, she was very much The Queen's Yacht, such was her personal involvement in the design. Unlike Sandringham, Balmoral or any of the other residences which The Queen inherited, *Britannia* provided an opportunity for Her Majesty to make her mark on the finished form. The Queen and Prince Philip had a final say in many aspects of the design, creating a Royal residence that truly reflected their tastes, interests and style.

Sir Hugh Casson, the co-ordinating architect for the 1951 Festival of Britain, was chosen as the designer for the Royal Apartments. His lightness of touch resulted in a simple elegance, which has stood the test of time.

66 *The Queen is a meticulous observer with very definite views on everything from the door-handles to the shape of the lampshades.* 99

Sir Hugh Casson

Casson's original interior sketch for the State Drawing Room

Casson's original interior sketch for the State Drawing Room Anteroom

Casson's original interior sketch for the State Dining Room

As a Naval Officer, Prince Philip took an active role in the technical aspects of the new Yacht. He also advised on which practices and traditions would be appropriate on a vessel fit for the 20th century.

Together, the Royal couple decided that the hull should be painted blue like their Dragon Class racing yacht *Bluebottle*, which had been given to them as a wedding present in 1948. This most visible aspect of *Britannia* set the new Yacht apart from her predecessors.

From broad aspects to small details, inside and out, *Britannia* became a living, floating reflection of the Royal personalities who would call her a home from home for the next 44 years.

One of the most striking features was the under-stated elegance of the Royal Apartments, reflecting the austerity of the post-war period when *Britannia* was built.

The first of several Royal Navy ships to be named *Britannia*, at the Battle of Barfleur, 1692 (*Britannia* is right of centre)

A long tradition

King Charles II's *Mary*

The German yacht *Grille*, rejected by King George VI as a suitable replacement for the ageing *Victoria & Albert III*

Britannia was the last of 83 Royal Yachts reaching back to 1660 and King Charles II's *Mary*, a gift from the people of Amsterdam.

Britannia's predecessor, *Victoria & Albert III*, was built for Queen Victoria and was the first Royal Yacht not to be powered at all by sail. However, the monarch was never to step aboard after hearing rumours about the Yacht's lack of stability. Queen Victoria's successor, King Edward VII, had no such qualms, although his voyages were largely confined to local waters and the Mediterranean. *Victoria & Albert III* was to serve four sovereigns before ending her service in 1939.

For longer voyages, the Admiralty would either charter a liner or convert a major warship for Royal use. Clearly, if a new Royal Yacht was to be built to meet the demands of an outward-looking Britain, with strong ties to the Commonwealth, she would need to have a truly global reach.

There was general agreement that it would be prudent for a new Royal Yacht to be capable of providing a secondary function during wartime. After some debate, it was agreed that a vessel capable of speedy conversion into a hospital ship should be built. However, this was a role *Britannia* never fulfilled, missing out on the Falklands Campaign because of logistical problems with the type of fuel she used, which would have necessitated her own dedicated fuel supply ship.

Victoria & Albert III

The binnacle rescued by Prince Phillip from
Victoria & Albert III, having previously been
relocated from Queen Victoria's *Royal George*

 The decision had been taken to scrap V&A (Victoria & Albert) so I travelled to Portsmouth to salvage various items including the two binnacles. All the silver, linen and glass was also transferred to Britannia.

HRH Prince Philip

Seven ships in the Royal Navy had carried the name *Britannia*, the first a 1703-ton warship dating back to 1682. Coincidentally, she finished her days as a hospital ship, the same role intended for the 'new' *Britannia* in time of war.

A Look Inside the Royal Yacht

1. Ensign Staff
2. Mizzenmast
3. Mainmast
4. Foremast
5. Jackstaff
6. Quarter Deck
7. The State Drawing Room
8. The Anteroom
9. Verandah Deck
10. The Sun Lounge
11. Royal Bedrooms
12. The Queen's Bathroom
13. The Queen's Bedroom
14. The Duke's Bedroom
15. The Duke's Bathroom
16. Maid's Room
17. Maid's Room
18. Wardrobe Room
19. Valet's Bedroom
20. The Queen's Sitting Room
21. The State Dining Room
22. Servery
23. Royal Household Cabins
24. Royal Household Cabins
25. Master of the Household's Cabin
26. The Equerry's Sitting Room
27. Cloak Room
28. Lower Entrance
29. Guest Suite
30. Junior Royal and VIP Cabins
31. Maid's Sitting Room
32. Royal Household Cabins
33. Royal Clerk's Office
34. Cypher Office
35. Main Turbine Engine Room
36. Baggage Rooms
37. Linen Store

38. Blanket Stores	51. Flag Deck	63. Laundry
39. Wine Stores	52. Royal Bridge	64. Yachtsmens' Mess
40. China Stores	53. Shelter Deck	65. Stabiliser Compartment
41. Fuel Tanks	54. Upper Deck	66. Engineers' Workshop
42. Dinghies	55. Anchor Cables & Capstans	67. Chief Petty Officer's Cabin
43. Fast Motor Launch	56. Air Conditioning Plant	68. Upper Mess
44. Royal Barge	57. Ship's Doctor's Room	69. Stokers' Mess
45. Activity Boat	58. Sick Bay & Operating Theatre	70. Cold Rooms
46. Jolly Boat	59. Boiler Rooms	71. Platform Deck
47. Compass Platform	60. Bathrooms	72. Capstan's Machinery Store
48. Officers' Cabins	61. Showers	73. Main Deck Mess
49. Radar Scanner	62. Generator Room	74. Lower Deck Store Rooms
50. Bridge		75. Shipwrights' Workshop

> " *This is where I can truly relax.* "
>
> HM The Queen

An informal dinner during The Queen's Silver Wedding Anniversary cruise in 1972

The grand staircase leading to the Shelter Deck where the Royal Bedroom suites are found

The Royal
Apartments

Two ships in one

*B*ritannia is really two ships in one. Forward of the mainmast is the operational side of the ship, where the Royal Navy Officers and Yachtsmen worked, and aft of the mainmast is where the Royal Apartments are situated.

The Royal Apartments in The Queen's other Royal residences, such as Buckingham Palace and Windsor Castle, are reserved for formal occasions. On *Britannia* the State Rooms within the Royal Apartments were used every day and it is here that The Queen's own preference for the understated is revealed.

With their collection of personal possessions, including family photographs and furnishings from previous Royal Yachts, the Royal Apartments truly reflect Her Majesty's desire that "*Britannia* is to be at times the home of my husband and myself and of our family."

The State Drawing Room has an air of informal elegance

The State Drawing Room and Anteroom

The State Drawing Room is the main reception room onboard *Britannia*. Next to this room is the smaller Anteroom where the Royal Family would assemble for drinks before lunch and dinner. Most of the furniture here was a gift from the Swedish Royal Family during a State visit to Stockholm in 1956. The antique mahogany bookcase and sideboard originate from the King's study in *Britannia's* predecessor, *Victoria & Albert III*. Taking pride of place in the bookcase, alongside the James Bond novels, is a set of Waterford crystal glasses and a tray presented by John Brown & Co, the shipyard that built *Britannia*.

The Anteroom is separated from the State Drawing Room by folding mahogany doors. The Drawing Room is large and comfortable, a place where the family could come together to relax with conversation, music and games. The Welmar grand piano is fastened to the floor by bolts in case of heavy weather. Probably the most notable name to 'sing for his supper' was Sir Noël Coward, invited to dine aboard during a Caribbean cruise by Princess Margaret.

The 17th century Waterford Crystal glasses, hand engraved by Laurence Whistler, presented to The Queen by John Brown & Co

The original plan for an open fire in the Drawing Room was scrapped due to a Naval regulation that a sailor would need to be stationed beside it with a bucket of water.

The overall idea was to give the impression of a country house at sea.

I think we succeeded. Even today the Yacht looks very striking. She

has an attractively old-fashioned air about her.

Sir Hugh Casson, 1984

The Anteroom with the bookcase from *Victoria & Albert III*

A portrait of Nelson hangs in the Anteroom

The Welmar grand piano in the State Drawing Room originally cost £350

At various other times, Diana, Princess of Wales, Princess Margaret and Princess Alexandra all entertained at the Welmar grand piano. For more formal occasions, a pianist from the Royal Marines Band provided suitably discreet background music. Cole Porter and Gershwin were particular favourites of The Queen.

Family entertainment centred around several card tables for bridge, whist or poker, as well as board games and the occasional large puzzle for the younger generation. A television set was housed in a specially-made cabinet, designed to blend in with the rest of the furniture.

The chintz sofas and armchairs, with covers originally chosen by The Queen, stand on a silver-grey carpet which runs the entire length of the Royal Apartments. It is partly covered by two stunning Persian rugs similar to those presented to The Queen during her visit to the Gulf States in 1979.

The State Dining Room also served as a place of worship on Sundays

The State Dining Room

The State Dining Room is the grandest room onboard *Britannia* and was the prestigious setting for hundreds of spectacular banquets. Many famous names accepted the invitation to dine with The Queen, including Churchill, Thatcher, Mandela, Reagan, Clinton and Yeltsin. The guest list is a long and illustrious one.

The original centrepiece of the room was the 32-seater mahogany table and its Hepplewhite chairs. The table was made in five sections to allow different configurations depending on the occasion. For full-scale State banquets, the seating could be increased by adding two tables which came from *Victoria & Albert III*. Also brought onboard from the previous Royal Yacht were four 19th century sideboards carved in the style of Chippendale. This furniture is now on display in The *Britannia* Room at Frogmore House, Windsor Castle.

For a State banquet the attention to detail would be meticulous. It could take up to three hours to set the dining table for 56 guests. The position of each item of cutlery and china was measured with a ruler to ensure perfection. Gracing the top table would be a pair of sculptured gold camels, said to be the single most valuable items onboard. They were given to The Queen by the Ruler of Dubai on her visit to the Gulf States in 1979.

The table settings are measured with a ruler to ensure perfection

Today, the menu is still carefully created for each occasion by *Britannia's* Executive Chef

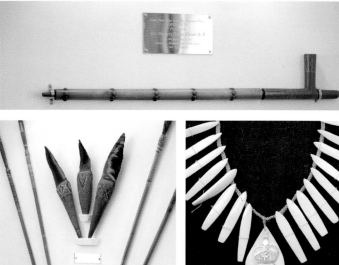

A selection of artefacts collected from all over the world are displayed on the State Dining Room walls

Presenting President and Mrs Reagan with a signed photograph, 1983

The whalebone collected by Prince Philip on Deception Island

The State Dining Room walls, painted white with a gold trim, display many interesting items including an array of exotic gifts and unusual mementoes of places visited. Some were given to The Queen, like a Sioux peace pipe from a visit to America, a sword dated 1738 given by the Swedish Navy, and a Narwhal tusk, a gift from the Prime Minister of Canada. Other curiosities were collected, such as the two-metre long whalebone, which Prince Philip found on a beach on Deception Island.

Each alcove around the room has its own story to tell, such as the one containing a wooden carving of a shark from Pitcairn Island. It is signed on the back by all the adults living there in 1971, descendants of Fletcher Christian, the leader of the *Bounty* mutiny.

In another alcove there are ceremonial swords and daggers presented to the Duke of Edinburgh in the Gulf States in 1979. Above these is the long red strip of feather money presented to the Duke in 1957 in Santa Cruz.

The State Dining Room was not only for entertaining; it also doubled as a cinema when on Royal duty and on Sundays was used for church services. In celebration of Princess Anne's upcoming 21st birthday the carpets were rolled up to reveal a hidden dance floor, which was put to good use for the first and probably last time on 2 August 1971.

The Queen's Sitting Room, where Her Majesty dealt with matters of State business

The wheatsheaf wall lights originally began life on *SS Gothic*

Headed notepaper as used by The Queen when aboard *Britannia*

The Queen's Sitting Room

On the starboard side, between the State Dining and Drawing Rooms, is The Queen's private Sitting Room. Here, Her Majesty worked at the green leather-topped desk for several hours a day on State papers brought to her in distinctive red boxes. These were flown or shipped out to *Britannia* wherever she happened to be in the world. It was also the place where The Queen held meetings with her Private and Press Secretaries, as well as approving Royal Yacht matters like the day's menus.

The original sofa and armchair were used in two previous Royal ships. The first was *HMS Vanguard* which took The Queen (then a young Princess) and her parents to South Africa. This was the first tour of South Africa by a reigning British monarch. The second was *SS Gothic*, the Shaw Savill merchant ship, which had been converted to be stand-in transport for the Coronation Tour of 1953.

Above the fireplace the striking ornate gilt mirror, in the style of a ship's wheel with carved figures of Neptune and a mermaid, began its life in The Queen's Drawing Room on the *SS Gothic*. The four wheatsheaf shaped wall lights, one in each corner of the room, have the same origin.

The Duke's Sitting Room

HRH Prince Philip's Sitting Room is on the port side. This 'study', as he preferred to call it, was also used by Prince Charles and, in contrast to The Queen's Sitting Room, has a masculine appearance with teak-panelled walls and a red leather-topped desk.

The Duke's Sitting Room was a convenient place for letter writing, quiet reading and meetings with his Private Secretary. Taking pride of place above the desk is a model of *HMS Magpie*, a reminder of the Duke's first naval command in 1951 when he was a Lieutenant Commander.

The model of *HMS Magpie* takes pride of place above The Duke's desk

The Duke's and The Queen's quarters were connected by telephone to each other and to their respective Private Secretaries in offices on the deck below. The telephone system used onboard was identical to that found at Buckingham Palace.

The Royal telephones, identical to those in Buckingham Palace

The Duke's Sitting Room with model of *HMS Magpie*

The Queen's Bedroom with its original 1950s furniture

The Royal Bedrooms

On the Shelter Deck are four bedrooms, including those of The Queen and The Duke of Edinburgh. The windows here are higher to prevent any accidental glances from those passing along the deck outside.

Both The Queen's and Prince Philip's bedrooms are on the starboard side, with a connecting door between them. Each has its own bathroom, complete with thermometer to ensure that the Royal bathwater was at the right temperature. Whilst both bedrooms are undoubtedly modest in decor, each has its own particular character: The Queen's with its floral charm and the Duke's with darker timber furniture.

The Queen's Bedroom features an embroidered silk panel with a floral motif above the bed, specially commissioned in 1953. Her Majesty's bed linen was from the *Victoria & Albert III*. The Duke's sheets were slightly smaller than The Queen's, who preferred a larger turnback, and on his explicit instructions were supplied with pillows that did not have lace borders.

The embroidered silk panel above The Queen's bed

Detail from Joan Nicholson's original watercolour design for the silk embroidery

Joan Nicholson, a young British designer, was chosen by Sir Hugh Casson to design the embroidered silk panel. The Queen wanted the embroidery to remind her of home when she was travelling abroad, with hedgerows, wild flowers and butterflies. Ivory silk from France was chosen for the background and it took several workers many months to complete at the Royal School of Needlework in London.

A connecting door links Prince Philip's and The Queen's bedrooms

Prince Philip's bedroom with a darker timber finish

The 'Honeymoon Suite', with the only double bed aboard *Britannia*

The Vestibule, flooded by warm morning light, connects the Royal Bedrooms and Sun Lounge

The grand staircase connects the Vestibule and the Royal Apartments below

Next to each bed is a panel with a buzzer to summon a steward should the need arise, day or night. During a state visit Her Majesty's Dresser could be very busy, with The Queen sometimes changing clothes up to five times a day. Her clothes, jewellery and accessories were kept in the wardrobe rooms on the same deck as the bedrooms. With the Prince being a Naval man, his particular concern was to ensure that the right medals or decorations were worn on every occasion.

There are two more bedrooms on the port side of the Shelter Deck, used by other members of the Royal Family. Probably the first people to use them were Prince Charles and Princess Anne as children. One of the rooms contains the only double bed onboard and was the accommodation for the four Royal honeymoon couples who spent the first days of their married life onboard *Britannia*.

Two decks below the Shelter Deck are a further sixteen cabins, each with its own en-suite facilities. Other members of the Royal Family, their guests and the Royal Household used these. The most senior guests, such as President and Mrs Clinton in 1994, were usually given the only suite of rooms on this level, namely Cabins 9 and 11, which are joined by a sitting room. The same suite was used by the last British Governor of Hong Kong, Mr Chris Patten, and his wife, on their return from the handover of Hong Kong in 1997.

Before a voyage, The Queen always approved the accommodation arrangements and would take particular care to ensure that special guests had suitable reading material for their bedside table and plenty of fresh flowers to decorate the room.

The Sun Lounge is beautifully lined in teak panelling

The Sun Lounge

Between the Vestibule and the Verandah Deck is The Queen's favourite room, the Sun Lounge, where she and her family would take afternoon tea.

With its comfortable sofas and bamboo and wicker chairs, it is a relaxed and informal room. Large picture windows provide spectacular views over the Verandah Deck and beyond. Cleverly concealed cupboards contain a refrigerated drinks cabinet and a record and games store. The line drawings of former Royal Yachts on these cupboard doors and the 'Rum Tot' tub dating from Queen Victoria's era are reminders of *Britannia's* glorious lineage.

The refrigerated drinks cabinet

The rum tub was used until 1970 to issue the Yachtsmen's daily rum ration

The Royal Family gathers on the Verandah Deck during the last Western Isles cruise in 1997

Prince Charles and his sons (Prince William and Prince Harry) by the compass binnacle, 1997

The Royal Coat of Arms

Britannia's Bell is the only place onboard to feature her full name

St Edward's Crown features at the top of the Binnacle

Verandah Deck

A short walk aft from the Royal Bedrooms through the Vestibule and the Sun Lounge is the wide expanse of the Verandah Deck, the scene of many happy family occasions: the Royal children splashing in a collapsible canvas swimming pool, Prince Philip painting at his easel, and games of quoits or deck hockey. It was also a ceremonial space, used for State receptions and entertaining guests in fine weather.

Whatever the occasion, a constant presence was the imposing figure of the ornate, intricately carved compass binnacle (originally carved from a single piece of teak). This was one of two rescued by Prince Philip from *Victoria & Albert III*, having previously been relocated from Queen Victoria's *Royal George*. It was a popular focal point for photographs taken by 'Snaps', the crew member who acted as photographer.

The Verandah Deck was reinforced to take the weight of a helicopter should *Britannia* have ever needed to fulfil her secondary role as a hospital ship. As it turned out, this was never put to the test.

The Royal
Photocall

Diana, Princess of Wales, rushes to greet her sons in Toronto, 1991

The Queen aboard *Britannia*, 1971

HM The Queen and HRH The Duke of Edinburgh are welcomed onboard The Royal Yacht *Britannia*

Younger members of the Royal Family on the Western Isles Cruise, 1997

Princes William and Harry give a royal wave, watched over by Rear Admiral Woodard, 1991

The Royal Family onboard *Britannia*, 1983

World Heads of State and Government pose for a photograph to commemorate D-Day, 1994

Royal flypast by Concorde, off Barbados, 1977

Mrs Thatcher comes aboard in Melbourne, 1981

The Queen Mother, Prince Charles and Princess Anne meet commanding officers before stepping onboard Britannia, 1954

Members of the Royal Family onboard Britannia, 1985

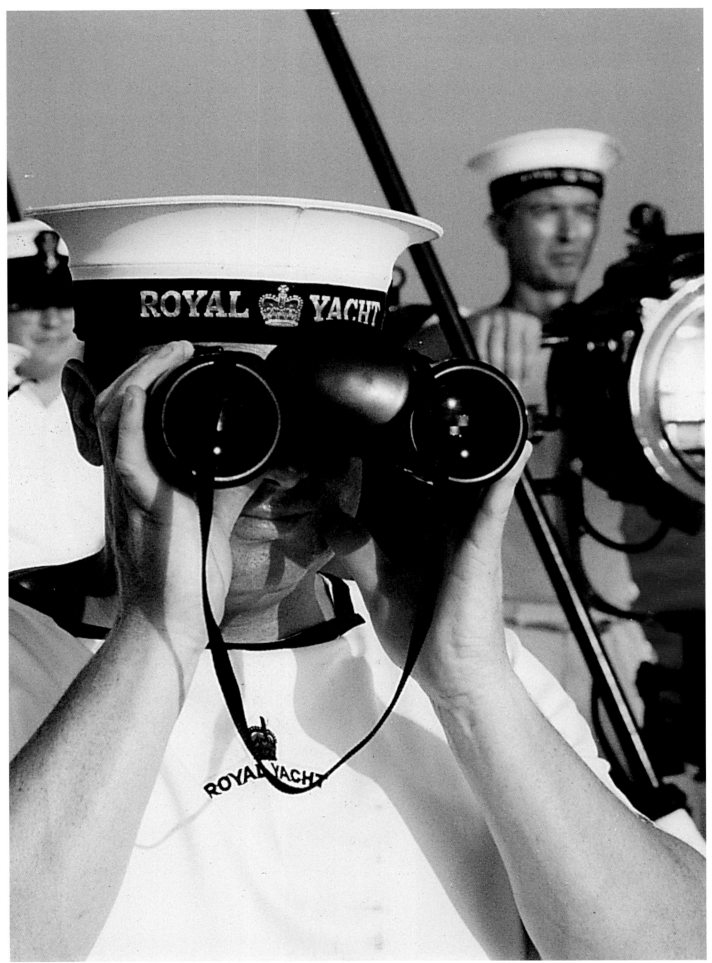

Signalling duty on the Flag Deck

Britannia's nerve centre, the Bridge

The Working Ship

The Bridge

The Bridge was the centre of command and control onboard *Britannia*. But unlike any other ship, the orders given and decisions taken here affected the safety and well-being of one of the most influential people in the world, HM The Queen.

Ultimately, overall responsibility rested with one man, *Britannia's* Captain. In recognition of this responsibility, *Britannia* was the only ship in the Royal Navy always commanded by a Flag Officer, generally a Rear Admiral. The one exception to the rule was the last Captain, Commodore Anthony Morrow.

When *Britannia* was at sea there would be an Officer of the Watch in overall charge, backed up by a Lookout and Signalman. Communication with the Helmsman on the deck below was via a metal voice pipe. To the rear of the Bridge is the Charthouse, where the Yacht's voyages were meticulously planned and plotted.

On the deck below is the Royal Bridge. Often, as *Britannia* sailed in or out of harbour, The Queen and The Duke of Edinburgh would wave to the cheering crowds on the quayside from here. The curved teak windbreak was a later feature, added for modesty's sake, to prevent sea breezes from lifting Royal skirts.

Metal voice pipe on the Bridge

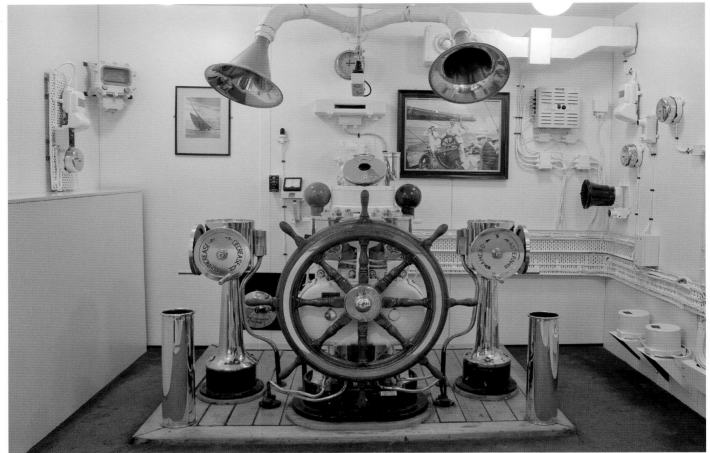

The Wheelhouse

The Wheelhouse

Britannia was steered and her engines controlled from the
Wheelhouse, with commands given via two voice pipes
from the Bridge. Normally, there would be three people
manning the Wheelhouse, one at the ship's wheel and two to
operate the brass telegraphs on either side of it. The telegraphs
were linked via mechanical rod gearing to the Engine Room five
decks below, passing on orders to regulate the ship's speed and
movement.

Britannia's wheel has an interesting history. It had originally
steered the racing yacht, also called *Britannia*, built for the Prince
of Wales (later King Edward VII) in 1893. It was then owned by
his successor, King George V, and upon his death, it was his wish
that his beloved *Britannia* be scuttled, however the wheel
was saved.

Britannia's wheel was originally from King Edward VII's racing yacht of the same name

Britannia's boats suspended from their overhead davits

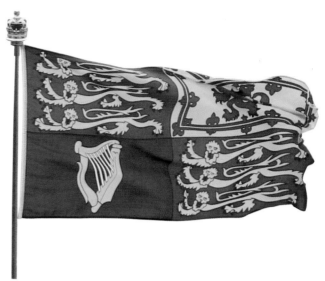

When The Queen was onboard, the mainmast flew the Royal Standard

The word *"Britannia"* shown in flags

The Flag Deck

Behind the Bridge on the Flag Deck, the Signalmen sent messages to other ships, either by hoisting signal flags with the halyards (ropes) or with Morse code flashed from the signal lights.

As a global traveller, not only did the Royal Yacht carry an average of 2,000 different flags, but a certain amount of raw bunting was kept handy should a little creative flag-making be required due to changes in or damage to national flags.

The most important flags were flown on the three main masts required by a Ship of State. When The Queen was onboard, the flag of the Lord High Admiral (The Queen) was flown at the foremast, the mainmast flew the Royal Standard and the mizzenmast displayed the Union flag.

Beneath the base of each of these hollow masts are two coins: a Coronation crown and shilling. These were placed when the masts were stepped (installed) in 1953. This was part of an age-old Naval custom when payment was made to the angels to protect the souls of the sailors.

The flag locker storing the signal flags

As *Britannia* would have had to travel under bridges, the top 20 feet of the mainmast and the radio aerial had to be hinged. This was a feature unique to *Britannia* at the time. The nautical term for this hinging manoeuvre is 'scandalising'.

The Admiral's day cabin is spacious and comfortable

The Admiral's Suite

Not only did the Admiral have ultimate responsibility for ensuring that *Britannia* ran like clockwork, but he was also in charge of a staff of some 21 Officers and 220 Yachtsmen. As befitted his standing, the Admiral's Suite contained the most spacious and comfortable rooms outside the Royal Apartments.

The Admiral's Suite is made up of a day cabin (with a sofa and armchairs from *Victoria and Albert III*), a sleeping cabin and a bathroom. The day cabin was for working, entertaining and sometimes eating meals. It was usual practice when The Queen, the Duke of Edinburgh or other members of the Royal Family were onboard for the Admiral to dine with them in the State Dining Room. When the Royal Family were not onboard, the Admiral tended to eat alone in his room so that the other Officers could unwind without feeling they had to be on their best behaviour in front of their boss. However, the Admiral did his fair share of entertaining too, hosting dinners or drinks parties for special guests.

The sycamore-veneered wardrobes in the Admiral's sleeping cabin held his uniforms; he sometimes had to change up to 12 times a day, depending on his duties.

The Admiral's sleeping cabin

BRITANNIA'S COMMANDING OFFICERS

Captain James Dalglish OBE RN	1954
Vice Admiral Sir Conolly Abel Smith, KCVO, CB	1954–1958
Vice Admiral Sir Peter Dawnay, KCVO, CB, DSC	1958–1962
Rear Admiral Sir Joseph Henley, KCVO, CB	1962–1965
Rear Admiral Sir Patrick Morgan, KCVO, CB, DSC	1965–1970
Rear Admiral Sir Richard Trowbridge, KCVO	1970–1975
Rear Admiral Sir Hugh Janion, KCVO	1975–1981
Rear Admiral Sir Paul Greening, GCVO	1981–1985
Rear Admiral Sir John Garnier, KCVO, CBE	1985–1990
Rear Admiral Sir Robert Woodard, KCVO	1990–1995
Commodore Anthony Morrow CVO RN	1995–1997

The Officers' Cabins were modest but comfortable

The First Lieutenant's Cabin

The Officers' Cabins

The Senior Officers' Cabins share a landing and corridor with the Admiral's Suite. The area was known as the 'Whispering Gallery', reflecting the need for quiet around their Commanding Officer. The Junior Officers' less spacious cabins were situated on the deck below.

The beds converted into sofas for use during the day and, as well as being sleeping quarters, the small cabins doubled as offices. Here Officers would write reports and store files, uniforms and personal possessions. There was no luxury of an en-suite bathroom, however, with facilities being shared.

Dinners in the Wardroom were formal occasions

The Wardroom

Step into the Officers' Wardroom and you are entering the equivalent of a gentlemen's club. Here, *Britannia's* 21 Officers would assemble to dine and relax in an atmosphere steeped in tradition.

Dinner in the Wardroom was a splendid affair with the Officers dressed in their 'Red Sea Rig' comprising a white shirt, black trousers, patent leather shoes and cummerbund. Pre-dinner drinks would be served in the Anteroom adjacent to the Wardroom. On more formal occasions Officers would take it in turns to say Grace, delivered in rhyme, often with a healthy dose of irreverence. The meal was always accompanied by fine wines from *Britannia's* extensive cellar. At the end of the meal the loyal toast to The Queen was made and, if present, the Royal Marines Band might play the National Anthem. As a final touch, the 'Youngest Unheard Officer' was sometimes invited to deliver an amusing speech.

In the glass cabinets around the Wardroom and in the adjacent Anteroom is a collection of 19th and 20th century objects, some from previous Royal Yachts, and many gifts from *Britannia's* Officers.

One of the objects, a silver Pegasus Bowl with flying horse handles depicting four previous Royal Yachts, was presented to the Wardroom by the Officers of *Victoria & Albert III*. From the same source came a small but immeasurably valuable object: a gold button taken from the uniform of Admiral Lord Nelson. Another relic comes from further afield – a large, very elaborate silver salt cellar in the form of a sailing ship, reputedly owned by Russia's last Czar.

The Pegasus Bowl depicts four former Royal Yachts

Precious metal: a small gold button from Nelson's coat hangs in the Wardroom Anteroom

The Wardroom Anteroom

Silver salt cellar from the last Russian Czar. The silver-work was so delicate it took a week to carefully clean

With the bar as its focus, the Anteroom was where the Officers could relax after the tension and discipline of being 'front of house' in the eyes of the Royal Family and a watching world. Drinks, listening to the radio, Yacht quizzes and some very boisterous games assisted the unwinding process.

'Wombat Tennis' was perhaps the most infamous of these games. The 'ball', a soft-toy wombat, was donated by one of The Queen's Ladies-in-Waiting. The match began when the wombat was 'served' up into the ceiling fan and then batted from one side of the room to the other. Needless to say, the poor wombat was a regular visitor to the Sick Bay where the Ship's Doctor would stitch it back together to face the next game.

Another creature to be found in various places around the room was a small wooden monkey. It arrived onboard when The Queen visited Copenhagen in 1957. It was said to be unlucky to find the monkey in the same place two days running, and so the Officers would wake to find the monkey in a new hiding place each day.

The 'Gin Pennant' was an important feature of the Anteroom. This was a small flag on a miniature flagstaff raised by an Officer to signal that the drinks were on him.

Besides the light-hearted fun and banter, the Anteroom did take on a more dignified atmosphere when the Officers entertained The Queen and the Duke of Edinburgh, or other members of the Royal Family, for dinner or a drinks party.

The Anteroom where Officers could relax and unwind

Warrant Officers' and Chief Petty Officers' Mess

In the Navy different ranks have their own recreation areas, known as Messes. As the most senior non-commissioned Yachtsmen onboard, the Warrant Officers and Chief Petty Officers had their own Mess with separate sleeping quarters. When *Britannia* took The Queen on her annual holiday around the Western Isles of Scotland, protocol was rather more relaxed, and occasionally The Queen and other members of the Royal Family would join the Chief Petty Officers here for a drink.

Set into the walls of the Mess are two alcoves that originally contained figures of two British seafaring legends: Sir Francis Drake and Admiral Lord Horatio Nelson. Like all of the other Messes, the walls here are lined with signed photographs of the Royal Family.

Warrant Officers' and Chief Petty Officers' Mess

Relaxing in the Petty Officers' and Royal Marines Sergeants' Mess

Petty Officers' and Royal Marines Sergeants' Mess

The Petty Officers and Royal Marines Sergeants had their own Mess with adjoining sleeping quarters. It was an extremely welcoming venue, so much so that an invitation to drink here was highly sought after by members of the Royal Household staff when they were onboard.

The Petty Officers' and Royal Marines Sergeants' Mess

The Royal Marines Band performs Beat Retreat

The cramped conditions of the Marines' Barracks

The Royal Marines' Barracks

The 26 musicians of the Royal Marines Band Service were *Britannia's* great entertainers. Their excellent musicianship and impeccable drill captured the imagination of audiences around the world.

Even President Reagan was moved to remark after viewing their 30-minute Beat Retreat ceremony on a Californian quayside: "Your Majesty, I thought Hollywood was the entertainment capital of the world, but there's no way we could beat this."

The Royal Marines also carried out other important duties. In their starched whites, they were most visible as sentries at the bottom of the gangway. They also held less public roles such as regularly diving beneath *Britannia's* hull, when in harbour, to check for anything suspicious.

The Marines' quarters (called 'Barracks') were extremely cramped with very little storage space, a real problem for the musicians who had to find space to store their uniforms and instruments, as well as personal belongings.

Stirring the Christmas pudding in *Britannia's* galley, 1991

The Galleys

On *Britannia* there are three Galleys: one for the Officers, one for the Yachtsmen and one for The Queen and Royal Household.

When the Royal Family was onboard, their food was always prepared by chefs from Buckingham Palace who were especially flown out to the ship. Before *Britannia* set sail, the ship's holds and store rooms were stocked with fresh, frozen and dried provisions. The cold rooms could hold two months' supply of fish and meat, and the dairy and vegetable rooms held enough provisions to feed the whole ship for a month. Fresh bread was baked daily, and whenever possible local vegetables were bought to supplement supplies.

There was a special cold room that was referred to as the 'Jelly Room', for it was in here that the Royal children's jellies were stored.

For formal occasions the three-course menus were usually printed long before the voyage began, but every morning The Queen would approve the day-to-day menus that were printed onboard.

The Galleys were capable of turning out large quantities of meals: a hundred chickens could be roasted simultaneously in the huge Admiralty ovens, whilst the enormous four-tiered steamer had no problem producing 200 puddings in a single batch.

The Silver Pantry

The China Pantry

The silverware gleams

EIIR

MENU

Gleneagles Pate

Suprême of Chicken with Wild Mushrooms
Salad

Chocolate and Ginger Mousse

WINES

Sancerre 1995
Château Arnauld 1990
Harveys Vintage Port 1983

TUESDAY 13TH MAY 1997   BANGKOK

Menu from Bangkok visit, 1997

Pantries

The China and Glass Pantry is where the Minton and Spode china for the State Dining Room was kept. Every cup, saucer, bowl and salt cellar has its own specially designed compartment, hook or rack to hold it. The glassware, some of which dates back to the reign of Edward VII, is all engraved with the royal cypher.

The Silver Pantry is located next door to the China and Glass Pantry. Much of the silver is Edwardian and with *Britannia's* exacting standards, every single item had to be polished daily.

The NAAFI

The original NAAFI

Today the NAAFI sells sweets and treats, including delicious fudge, made onboard

The NAAFI (Navy, Army and Air Force Institute) was the onboard shop. Open to everyone, it stocked basics such as confectionery, toothpaste, tobacco and a range of souvenirs unique to the Royal Yacht. These ranged from cut-glass whisky decanters and matching glasses to more modest T-shirts, pens and plaques, all bearing the *Britannia* crest and name.

The Royal children often visited to stock up on sweets. Diana, Princess of Wales, once bought a pale blue *Britannia* T-shirt for Prince William.

This shop onboard still trades and is part of the tour. It sells fudge (made onboard), sweets, drinks and gifts, which are greatly enjoyed by visitors.

The original NAAFI sign, still in use today

The Mail Office

Britannia was away from home for long stretches, often voyaging to the other side of the world, and her Mail Office provided a vital service for keeping in touch with family and friends. These were the days before mobile phones, so wherever *Britannia* berthed, the arrival of the mailbags was eagerly awaited by the Yachtsmen.

When The Queen was onboard, her official mail would be flown or shipped out from London to *Britannia* every day. Then, the ship's mail would join the 'Royal Mail' and the Officers and Yachtsmen could send and receive post daily via the Buckingham Palace Court Postmaster.

The Mail Office, a vital link with family and friends

Britannia's Laundry was far larger than that of other Navy ships of a similar size

The laundry was permanently manned by her own crew

The Laundry

There were two reasons why the Royal Yacht was the only ship in the Royal Navy to have such a large Laundry, permanently manned by her own crew.

Firstly, if ever converted into a hospital ship, there would be a need for greater capacity than normal. Secondly, with *Britannia's* 241 Officers and Yachtsmen changing uniform up to six times a day when on Royal duty, there was clearly a need to deal with an enormous amount of laundry. The washing machines, dryers and steam presses used to work around the clock. Up to 600 shirts could be processed in a single day.

The Laundry also took care of the Royal washing, although a strict rota kept this separate from the Yachtsmen's clothes. On one occasion the Royal washing turned an unexpected shade of blue (and Her Majesty's Dresser turned an angry shade of purple). The cause was quickly traced to a chemical reaction in the pipes, remedied by adjusting the pH value of the water.

This was a very uncomfortable place to work, with temperatures rising as high as 45° Celsius (120° Fahrenheit). It certainly made an impression on Prince Charles: "I always admired those characters who worked in such heat".

The Sick Bay and Operating Theatre

When the plans for the Royal Yacht were approved by The Queen early in 1952, they incorporated the idea that *Britannia* should be able to be converted to a hospital ship during times of conflict. It was estimated that up to 200 patients could be accommodated in wards in the aft part of the ship where the Royal Apartments were located.

A dental surgery, anaesthetic rooms and X-ray equipment, as well as other specialist facilities such as a physiotherapy room and a pathology laboratory, were also planned. The objective was to convert from Royal Yacht to hospital ship in a mere 24 hours.

In 1992, it was finally decided that the casualty and medical care needs of a modern Navy could be better met elsewhere and therefore this secondary role for the Royal Yacht ceased.

The Yacht's regular medical facilities incorporated a Sick Bay with accommodation for two patients in cot-beds and another two bunks contained within a bench seat. There was also a Doctor's Consulting Room and an Operating Theatre. The Ship's Doctor, who was usually also an anaesthetist, would look after the health of the Officers and Crew, whilst The Queen always had a Royal Navy Surgeon accompany her on overseas tours.

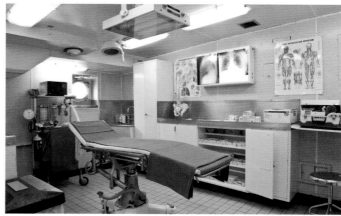

The Operating Theatre

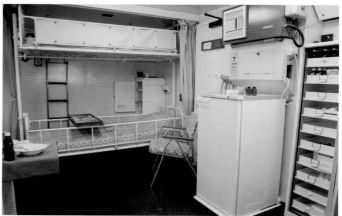

The Sick Bay

Pressure gauges

Britannia's Engine Room was kept immaculately clean

HM The Queen's royal insignia features in The Engine Room

The Engine Room, Generator and Boiler Rooms

This Engine Room is quite unlike any other. It had a mat outside, not to wipe one's feet when leaving, but to do so when entering. The immaculate world of white enamel, polished chrome, brass and gleaming black steam turbines has barely changed since 1953. Little wonder that during his visit to *Britannia* in 1992, America's General Schwarzkopf was heard to remark, "Okay, I've seen the museum piece. Now, where's the real Engine Room?"

The engines have steamed 1,087,623 nautical miles, with barely a problem. They turned out a total of 12,000 horsepower and drove Britannia, with her twin four-bladed propellers, to a maximum of 22.5 knots. However, she normally cruised at approximately 14 knots.

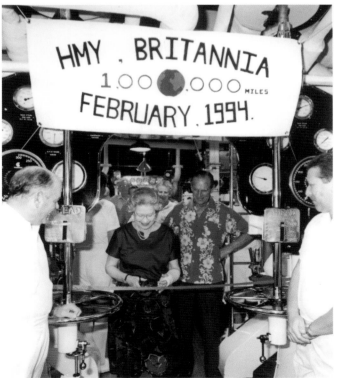
The Queen cuts a ribbon to celebrate the One Millionth Mile ceremony, 1994

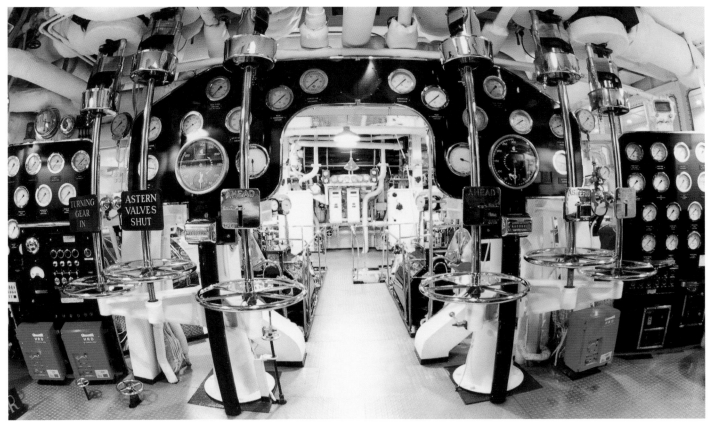

The Boiler Room supplied the steam which drove *Britannia*'s turbines

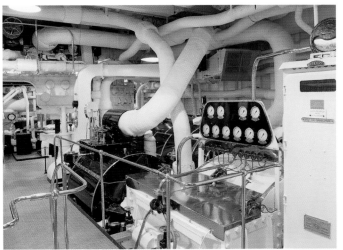

Two pairs of steam turbines powered *Britannia*

Britannia's electricity needs could be satisfied by any two of the three turbo generators

The Boiler Room next to the Engine Room was where the power for the Royal Yacht was generated. A pair of Foster Wheeler 'D' Type boilers initially burned furnace fuel before being converted to diesel in 1983. From here, the steam passed through large white pipes to drive the Engine Room's turbines. Their power went to the gearboxes, which drove the ship's propellers via 30 metre-long shafts.

Electricity for the Yacht came from a trio of turbo-steam generators. Back-up emergency power could be provided by a diesel generator (nicknamed 'Chitty Chitty Bang Bang'), rumoured to have been the oldest in active service in the entire Royal Navy. This generator originally drove HM Submarine *Vampire*.

This was not the only piece of equipment with a history: some of the water distillers were from the battleship *HMS Queen Elizabeth* which took part in the Dardanelles Campaign of 1915.

 Visitors to the Engine Room invariably ask to see the 'golden rivet', said to be secretly driven into every great ship in the dead of night. To satisfy their curiosity, one was improvised with the application of gold leaf on an existing rivet.

The Rolls-Royce in its transporter

The Garage

When *Britannia* was built in 1953, a garage to house The Queen's Rolls-Royce Phantom V or the Royal Land Rover (for Western Isles excursions) was considered an absolute essential. However, it was not a straightforward task to get a vehicle onboard. The car, in its transporter, had to be hoisted onto a special track that was fitted into the deck. Even then, the Rolls-Royce could only be squeezed into the Garage by removing its bumpers. In more recent times a suitable car could usually be found in the country that The Queen was visiting, so the Rolls-Royce was rarely carried and the Garage was put to use as a beer store.

Hoisting the Rolls-Royce onboard was a complicated procedure

The Land Rover being carefully hoisted onboard

The Royal Barge taking part in the Thames Diamond Jubilee Pageant, 2012

The Royal Barge

When *Britannia* was anchored in harbours around the world, The Queen and Prince Philip would use the Royal Barge to travel to shore. The air-conditioned cabin was specially designed to ensure that the Royal party could be clearly seen as they approached the shore.

The Barge was built by Camper Nicholson in 1964 to replace the previous Royal Barge, which had originally belonged to the Royal Yacht *Victoria and Albert III*. It is 12.5 metres long and has two 125 horsepower engines which are capable of a maximum speed of 20 knots. When The Queen was onboard the Royal Barge, she would be escorted by the Barge Officer, with a crew of five Royal Yachtsmen.

With a total of 10 boats and 18 life rafts, *Britannia* carried more craft than a warship. The 'activity boat' was often used to take the Royal Family ashore for private picnics and a fast motor boat was used to escort the Royal Barge whenever The Queen was onboard.

The Royal Barge was used to take The Queen and Prince Philip ashore

Plotting a course

A crew apart

Britannia's 21 Officers and 220 Royal Yachtsmen, known as 'Yotties', were part of the Royal Navy, but in many ways they were apart from it – in ethos, custom and practice. After all, this was no ordinary vessel: constantly in the public eye, charged with the security of the Royal Family and dedicated to achieving 'unobtrusive excellence' in everything she did. This took absolute attention to detail with little or no room for error, which included taking three hours to set the table with inch-perfect precision for a State banquet, or ensuring that the slope of the Royal gangway never exceeded 12 degrees.

Everything was done to preserve the Royal tranquillity. Consequently, most orders were not given verbally, but by hand signal; soft soled plimsolls were worn and any work near the Royal Apartments had to be completed by 08:00.

Around half of the ship's company were appointed for a two-year tour of duty. The rest of the Royal Yachtsmen were hand-picked for permanent service and remained with *Britannia* throughout their Naval career, accepting this post for the honour and privilege of serving The Queen.

Service on the Royal Yacht attracted no extra pay, allowances or leave. There was not much chance of promotion either, as this was only possible if someone left the Royal Yacht Service, which was extremely rare. Yachtsmen could also face instant dismissal for misconduct.

Even when they were ashore, the Royal Yachtsmen were set apart, having to wear collar and tie after 18:30. In contrast to this formality, all ratings were called by their first names (or nicknames). And there was the opportunity to join in the traditional end-of-cruise concert party in front of the Royal Family.

If any urgent changes were made to the daily orders that regulated every minute of life onboard, they would be posted on the 'red-hot' notice boards throughout the Yacht. Woe betide any crewman who did not pay close attention.

The Queen with some 'Yotties', South Pacific Tour, 1977

A rare moment of mass relaxation during The Queen's 1961 cruise to Africa

" *My abiding memory is not of places, but of people, the Royal Yachtsmen, a ship's company who have no equal. I felt I could call on them to do anything and it would be done, cheerfully, efficiently and quietly.* "

Lord Lewin

Principal
Medical Officer
(PMO)

 1 Chief Petty Officer (CPO)
Medical Assistant
*In charge of Sick Bay routine &
assistant to PMO*

1 CPO Medical Technician
Physiotherapist

Medical Department

 Director of Music

 Colour Sergeant
The Drum Major

Colour Sergeant
The Bandmaster

5 Sergeant
Bandsmen

8 Corporal
Bandsmen

6 Bandsmen

Royal Marines Band Service

 Admiral
(Commodore)

 Commander N
*Navigation &
Communications*

 Assistant
Navigation &
Meteorology
Officer

 Communications
& Royal Cypher
Officer

 1 CPO Chief
Radio Superviser
*In charge of Radio
Sub-Department*

1 CPO Chief
Communications
Yeoman
*In charge of Tactical
Signalling*

2 PO Radio
Supervisers

1 Petty
Officer (PO)
Communications
Yeoman
*In charge of Flag
Deck & Message
Distribution*

2 Leading Radio
Operators
*Tactical Signalling
Sub-Department*

3 Leading Radio
Operators
*Radio Sub-
Department*

Navigation Department

 The Commander
*Executive Officer
& second in
command.*

 1 First Lieutenant
Fo'c's'le Officer

1 Second
Lieutenant
Quarterdeck Officer

 1 The Boatswain
(Bo's'n)
*In charge of
Britannia's Boats*

1 The Royal
Barge Officer
*Also serves as
Household Liaison
Officer*

 1 Chief Bo's'n's
Mate
*In charge
of Seaman
Department
Activity*

1 Coxswain
*In charge of
Discipline &
Administration*

 The Queen's
Coxswain
*In charge of the
Royal Barge*

1 Waist PO

1 Fo'c's'le PO

1 Quarterdeck
PO

1 Chief
Quartermaster &
Routines PO

Seaman Department

 Commander E
*The Engineer
Commander &
Wardroom Mess
Secretary*

 Senior Engineer
*Deputy to
Commander E*

 1 Main Machinery
Officer
*In charge of main
machinery*

1 Outside Machinery
Officer
*In Charge of auxilliary
machinery, shipwrights
& laundry*

1 Electrical Officer

 Warrant Officer
*In charge of logistics
& personnel.*

3 CPO Marine
Engineering Mechanics
In charge of Boiler Room

1 CPO Engineer Articifer
*In charge of auxiliary
machinery*

2 CPO Engineer
Shipwrights

2 CPO Engineer
Artifacers

1 CPO Electrician

 5 Petty Officer
Marine Engineer
Mechanics
*With Part of Ship
responsibilities*

Engineering Department

 Commander S
*The Supply Officer &
Admiral's Secretary*

 The Keeper
& Steward
of the Royal
Apartments

 Deputy Supply
Officer
*Deputy to
Commander S*

 Warrant Officer
Writer
*In charge of pay &
the Admiral's office*

 1 CPO Steward
*In charge of the
Wardroom*

1 CPO Caterer
*In charge of
catering & menu
planning*

2 CPO Stewards
Shipwrights
*Deputy & Assistants
Keepers & Stewards
of the Royal
Apartments*

 1 CPO Cook
*In charge of the
Royal & Wardroom
Galleys*

1 CPO Cook
*In charge of the
Ship's Galley*

Supply Department

4 Buglers

4 Radio
Operators
*Tactical Signalling
Sub-Department*

6 Radio
Operators
*Radio Sub-
Department*

1 Navigator's
Yeoman

Who's who in *Britannia*

As with all Royal Navy Ships, the Captain (Admiral or Commodore in *Britannia's* case) was in charge, supported by his staff of up to 21 Officers and 220 Yachtsmen. However, *Britannia's* complement could vary depending on the Yacht's duties.

Royal Marine
Colour Sergeant
*In charge of
Royal Marines
Detachment*

Physical Training
Instructor
*Also in charge of
between decks*

3 Leading
Seamen

1 Fo'c's'le
Leading Seaman

1 Quarterdeck
Leading Seaman

24 Able
Seamen

4 Royal Marines
*Part of Ship (Royal
Deck), also Royal
Marines Orderlies
& Security Sentries*

Commander's
Office Writer
*In charge of
producing
programmes, Daily
Orders & Red Hot
Notices*

1 Petty Officer
*In charge of the
Laundry*

7 Leading
Marine Engineer
Mechanics
*With Part of Ship
responsibilities*

24 Marine
Engineer
Mechanics
*With Part of Ship
responsibilities*

8 Laundry Crew

3 Wardroom Leading
Stewards

1 Admiral's Leading
Steward

3 Leading Stores'
Accountants

1 Leading Writer

4 Leading Stewards

1 Leading Airman
Photographer 'Snaps'

2 PO Stewards
In the Wardroom

1 PO Naval Stores

1 PO Cook
Wardroom Galley

1 PO Cook
Ship's Galley

2 Wardroom
Leading Cooks

2 Ship's Galley
Leading Cooks

4 Wardroom
Cooks

4 Ship's
Galley Cooks

Royal
Marine
Butcher

8 Wardroom
Stewards

2 Writers
*Admiral's
Office*

8 Royal
Stewards

Peter Phillips lends a hand slipping anchor

Princess Anne has a Royal Yacht 'sailing' lesson, 1954

A Royal Residence

66

We found as children that there was so much to do, we expended so much energy that we couldn't describe our time in the Yacht as a rest.

99

HRH Princess Anne

The young Princes Andrew and Edward, Viscount Linley and Lady Sarah Armstrong-Jones practice their saluting

A floating nursery

From practically her first voyage, *Britannia* became a playground for generations of Royal children. It was customary for each Royal child to be allocated at least one minder from the crew to look after them while onboard. The ship's company ensured that there was never a shortage of amusements including treasure hunts, picnics ashore and water fights using syringes from the sick bay.

However, even the patience of the most dedicated Yachtsman was tried when a young Prince Charles kicked his football over the side off the Isle of Man, not just once, but twice. Needless to say, *Britannia* didn't turn back to collect it the second time.

It wasn't all play though. The Royal children had their 'chores' to do too: helping to clean life rafts, stirring the ship's enormous Christmas pudding and even taking a (highly supervised) hand at the wheel.

Appropriately enough on a Yacht so familiar with ceremony, the young Princes Andrew and Edward and their cousins, Viscount Linley and Lady Sarah Armstrong-Jones, tried out as Officers. However, their Naval saluting left much to be desired, having been copied from the guards at Buckingham Palace.

After the fun of the day, the Royal children had their meals separately from the adults – even at that early age they were learning the formality and etiquette that was to become second nature in later life.

Britannia at the Cowes Week Regatta in 1996

Cowes Week and the annual Western Isles cruise

The Royal summer plans followed a well-established pattern and *Britannia* played a key role. The Royal Yacht would first appear at the Cowes Week Regatta off the Isle of Wight, where Prince Philip and other members of the Royal Family would exercise their passion for yacht racing. Then *Britannia* would set sail for the Western Isles of Scotland for The Queen's annual holiday cruise. While the Royal Family was cruising, the Royal Household would move from Buckingham Palace to their northern home at Balmoral to prepare for the arrival of The Queen and her family.

Visiting the outlying parts of western Scotland on a leisurely cruise away from the crowds allowed The Queen and her family to relax and unwind. It meant barbeques ashore on deserted beaches, quiet walks and informal concert parties organised by the Yachtsmen.

Another traditional part of the cruise was to anchor off Scrabster, in order to visit The Queen Mother at the Castle of Mey. It was also a time when The Queen would invite the Officers to dine with her. The Officers would reciprocate with a dinner for The Queen and Prince Philip in the Wardroom.

The Queen, Prince Andrew and Prince Edward wave as they leave Portsmouth at the start of the Western Isles cruise in 1991

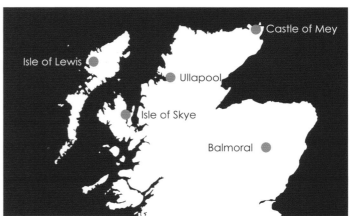

The Western Isles, situated on the West Coast of Scotland

Sharing a joke off the Isle of Mull

The Queen Mother greets The Queen at Scrabster harbour, 1996

"*She (The Queen) got a week or ten days of sanctuary from anything that was going on. That little bit of tranquillity made up for all the other things that she had to do... it was a chance to have her family around her in her environment.*"

The Duke of York

Princess Anne takes a photograph while on honeymoon with Captain Mark Phillips, 1973

Honeymoon hideaway

There could not have been a more ideal venue for a Royal honeymoon. Secluded from the public eye and able to cruise to out-of-the-way places, *Britannia* played host to four Royal honeymoons.

The first newlyweds, Princess Margaret and Anthony Armstrong-Jones, visited the West Indies in 1960 for a month, anchoring off small islands and enjoying picnics ashore.

In 1973 Princess Anne and Captain Mark Phillips also chose the Caribbean for their honeymoon. With the world's press dogging their every move, the Yacht's company had their work cut out to ensure the privacy of the Royal couple. On more than one occasion, they resorted to the ruse of sending a decoy barge to a beach to throw the press photographers off the trail.

The first honeymooners: Princess Margaret and Anthony Armstrong-Jones, 1960

Princess Anne's honeymoon cruise got off to a rocky start with twenty-foot waves sending the Royal couple to their bed with a bad case of seasickness.

The Prince and Princess of Wales on their honeymoon, 1981

> " *I was in the scullery washing up when I heard a voice in the servery. I went out to look, to find a newly-wed Princess sitting on the freezer in a bikini, flip flops and hat, licking a choc ice.* "

Leading Steward Mark Elliot

In 1981, the Prince and Princess of Wales boarded *Britannia* in Gibraltar to begin their 16-day honeymoon around the Mediterranean. It was a thoroughly informal time, at least as far as the young Princess was concerned. She enjoyed exploring the lower decks and, on one notable occasion, joined the Yachtsmen in an impromptu sing-song, including 'What shall we do with the drunken sailor?'

It was five years later that *Britannia*'s final honeymoon cruise took her to the Azores. Onboard were The Duke and Duchess of York. Once again, the press were kept at bay and the time spent together aboard *Britannia* made for happy memories: "After all the organisation of the things that we had to do, to be able to have four or five days of complete peace and quiet was fantastic", The Duke recalled.

The perfect romantic retreat

An
Ambassador's *Role*

"

On the jetty, there was a huge crowd and there were bands playing. Suddenly, around the Spithead came the sight of this amazing ship with the Royal Marines Band playing on the top deck, flags flying, and The Queen and the Duke of Edinburgh on deck waving to the crowds. It was so proud-making, beautiful and British.

"

Lady Susan Hussey, The Queen's Lady-in-Waiting

On the Royal Bridge with President Eisenhower during the opening of the St Lawrence Seaway in 1959

Meeting President Mandela in Cape Town, 1995

Britain afloat

*B*ritannia was the first, and indeed the last, truly global Royal Yacht. Wherever in the world she went, a little bit of Britain went too. During almost 44 years of service, *Britannia* made over 700 overseas visits to just about every corner of the globe. From the Amazon River to the St Lawrence Seaway, from the South Sea Islands to New York City, *Britannia* was a powerful symbol of Britain and all it stood for.

For citizens of the Commonwealth, who saw *Britannia* a total of 223 times, the Royal Yacht was both a link with their colonial past and a reminder of their ongoing relationship with the United Kingdom. As The Queen herself remarked at the launch, speaking of her late father: "For he felt most strongly, as I do, that a yacht was a necessity and not a luxury for the Head of our great British Commonwealth, between whose countries the sea is no barrier, but the natural and indestructible highway."

For many citizens of far-flung Commonwealth countries, the distinctive blue-hulled presence of *Britannia*, gleaming and immaculate from bow to stern, was as close to a vision of Britain as they could ever hope to see.

Britannia in the sunshine off the Cayman Islands, 1994

How do you arrive gleaming in port after a long sea voyage? Make sure you head for the nearest rainstorms en route, rinsing off the salt and leaving beautifully shining sides.

Prince Charles is met by His Highness, the Crown Prince in Doha, Qatar, 1997

Royal returns

As the pressure to justify the costs of maintaining a Royal Yacht grew more acute, it was felt that *Britannia* should play a more commercial role as a venue for British overseas trade missions. An invitation to come onboard for what became known as 'Sea Days' proved irresistible to the world's leading business and political figures, especially on those occasions when a member of the Royal Family was present.

A British businessman bidding for part of a £4 billion Chinese steel contract vividly described one example of *Britannia*'s unique attraction to Rear Admiral Garnier, "He told me that all the people he wanted to see were on his table, including the relevant Chinese Government Minister, the Mayor and the Project Manager … it would have taken him another six months to a year to have done that without a Sea Day!"

From the very first Sea Day in Rio in 1968, to the final one hosted in Gibraltar on 22 July 1997, *Britannia*'s allure earned Britain and its companies a very healthy return. Commercial contracts are generally too confidential for a precise figure, but the Overseas Trade Board estimated that £3 billion had been made for the Exchequer as a result of commercial days between 1991 and 1995 alone. As the ultimate in 'networking' venues, *Britannia* had clearly proved her status as an invaluable asset on the UK's trade balance sheet.

Princess Alexandra presents an award during an investiture in Tokyo, 1997

Britannia *was invaluable for this kind of event. We wanted to have the top business leaders in attendance and an invitation to dinner on the Royal Yacht was seldom refused, particularly when spouses were included.* ”

Lord Michael Forsyth

Commodore Anthony Morrow escorts Margaret Beckett, Minister for Trade and Industry, on her visit to *Britannia* in Japan, 1997

Britannia's boats pick up evacuees from Aden, South Yemen

Mercy mission

After 30 years of service, *Britannia* had yet to fulfil her secondary role as a hospital ship. However, as she sailed down the Red Sea in January 1986, en route to Australia, she was asked to play the equally challenging role of rescue ship. Civil war had broken out in South Yemen and ships were urgently required to evacuate British nationals and others trapped by the fighting. As a non-combatant Royal Navy ship, *Britannia* would be able to enter territorial waters without further inflaming the conflict. The Queen swiftly gave her full backing and the State Dining and Drawing Rooms were cleared to welcome a new type of guest.

At 20:00 on 17 January 1986, the Yacht, with a large Union flag flying at each mast and her superstructure floodlit so no-one could mistake her identity, dropped anchor off Khormaksar Beach. The first of *Britannia's* boats headed for shore to begin the shuttle of evacuees back to the refuge of the Royal Yacht.

After being given a blanket, hot soup and a snack, the refugees were shown to dormitories improvised within the State Apartments. Over the next six days, the Yacht's boats rescued 1,068 of the 1,379 people of 55 nationalities saved by British ships during what became known as Operation Balsac. Often operating under fire from the opposing sides, her crew thoroughly deserved the telegrams of praise that later streamed in from The Queen, the Prime Minister, the Foreign Secretary and all the defence chiefs.

The White Ensign

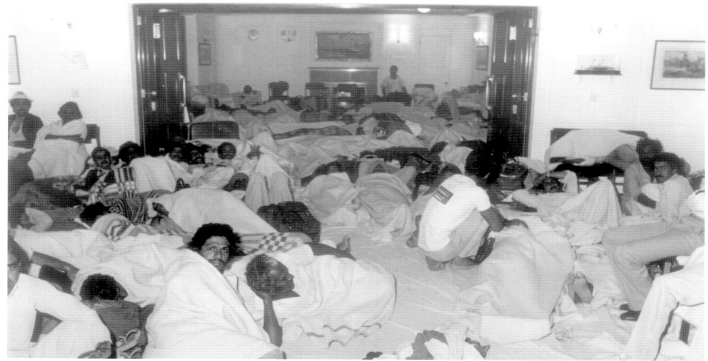

The State Drawing Room and Anteroom welcome a new type of guest

" *When I saw the launch coming in, with its White Ensign fluttering in the wind, I was*
very happy inside and there were tears in my eyes. The Queen's Yacht turned back for
me, just for me! "

Yemen-born London bus driver, Saleh Ali

British evacuees from Aden arrive safely back in Britain

For the last time, *Britannia* sails into Portsmouth

Final Voyage

" *Looking back over forty-four years we can all reflect with pride and gratitude upon this great ship which has served the country, the Royal Navy and my family with such distinction. Britannia has provided magnificent support to us throughout this time, playing such an important role in the history of the second half of this century.* "

HM The Queen

A long goodbye

Hong Kong marked *Britannia's* last official visit to a foreign port

B *ritannia's* final and most widely televised role was at the handing over of Hong Kong, at the stroke of midnight on 30 June 1997. After the Union flag (Union Jack) was lowered for the last time, she slipped out of Hong Kong Harbour carrying the last Governor, Chris Patten. With her final Royal duty completed, this symbol of the British Commonwealth could head back to home waters for the last time.

In June 1994, Rear Admiral Woodard announced to the whole ship's company in the State Dining Room that the Conservative Government had decided *Britannia* was to be decommissioned. On 10th October 1997, the new Labour Government announced that there would be no replacement for *Britannia*. However, she was to be preserved as a national treasure and not scuttled as was the tradition for Royal Yachts.

In the years leading up to 1997, there had been rumours that a new Royal Yacht might be commissioned. Political opinion had been mixed. The argument for *Britannia's* trade role was made by some. The Ministry of Defence had actually been considering some fairly advanced plans, with an estimated construction bill of £80 million.

Chris Patten leaves Hong Kong with the Union flag under his arm

Commodore Anthony Morrow watches as Prince Charles greets Tony Blair before the handover of Hong Kong

The final shut down of the engines, November 22 1997

The Queen leaves the Royal Yacht for the very last time in Portsmouth, 11 December 1997

Decommissioning

On 20 October 1997, *Britannia* left Portsmouth on her final operation: a farewell tour of the UK. In a clockwise circumnavigation of Britain, *Britannia* visited six major ports, including Glasgow.

Having said her goodbyes, *Britannia* hoisted the traditional paying-off pennant. This usually measures one and a half times the length of the ship plus one foot for every year of service, but as this would have been too unwieldy it was decided to make it 412 feet, the Yacht's length.

With pennant flying in a dramatic thunderstorm, the last Royal Yacht sailed from London on 21 November 1997 for a final night at sea as she headed for her decommissioning port, Portsmouth. She docked the next morning and at 11:35am, the Engine Room heard their last orders as the call came to stop engines. *Britannia's* Royal career was over.

On 11th December 1997, The Queen, accompanied by the vast majority of the Royal Family, attended *Britannia's* decommissioning ceremony in Portsmouth. As the band marched off for the final time, they struck up 'Auld Lang Syne' and saluted the Yacht.

Many a tear was shed, not just by The Queen and The Princess Royal, but also by more than one hard-bitten former Yachtsman. As The Queen's Private Secretary put it: "It was a very moving occasion because everyone was saying good-bye to something they all loved, from The Queen downwards."

All the clocks onboard *Britannia* remain stopped at one minute past three; the exact time The Queen was piped ashore for the final time

Saying farewell to *Britannia* was emotional for everyone

The first ever ship's company with The Queen, Prince Philip, Prince Charles and Princess Anne in 1954

The last ever ship's company with The Queen and Prince Philip, taken before *Britannia's* decommissioning in 1997

Britannia,
the last *Royal Yacht*

On 11 December 1997, at precisely one minute past three in the afternoon,
The Queen was piped ashore for the final time from Britain's last Royal Yacht.
44 years earlier, The Queen had stood on a raised platform high above the
Clydebank shipyard of John Brown & Co and pressed the button that launched
Ship Number 691 into the Clyde.

Between those two occasions stretched an illustrious history of service that took
Britannia the equivalent of once around the world for every year she sailed and
made her the most famous ship afloat.

Britannia played host to the world's elite and was a powerful draw to the crowds
who admired her wherever she went. In public, she was a living, working symbol
of Royal Britain, whilst in private, away from the public eye, *Britannia* was the
perfect sanctuary for The Queen and her family.

Britannia at the Tower Bridge Centenary Celebrations, 1994

Together with members of my family, Prince Philip and I join you today to pay tribute to BRITANNIA and give our thanks to all who have been part of her Company. Looking back over forty-four years we can all reflect with pride and gratitude upon this great ship which has served the country, the Royal Navy and my family with such distinction. BRITANNIA has provided magnificent support to us throughout this time, playing such an important role in the history of the second half of this century. Steaming over one million miles she has proudly carried out over seven hundred Royal visits at home and overseas as well as numerous highly successful commercial programmes. Her achievements are a great testament to those who designed and built her and to those craftsmen and artisans who have maintained her with such dedication over all these years.

In recognising BRITANNIA's marvellous service, we pay particular tribute to the Officers and Royal Yachtsmen who have served in her. My family and I extend our heartfelt thanks to all these men for their unfailing loyalty, dedication and commitment to the Royal Yacht Service. While many of the present Royal Yacht's Company will return to the Royal Navy to continue their naval service and others come to the end of their service, we wish you every success in your future endeavours. We would also wish to thank the wives and families who have quietly but strongly supported the Royal Yacht over the years and often during the periods of long absence.

It is with sadness that we must now say goodbye to BRITANNIA. It is appropriate that with this final event she bows out in the style which is so typical of the manner in which her business has always been conducted.

Elizabeth R   *Philip*

11th December 1997.

A New Life
for *Britannia*

Britannia berthed in the historic port of Leith

Moving to Edinburgh

In the lead-up to HMY *Britannia's* decommissioning, the Government invited UK organisations to bid to provide a new home for the Royal Yacht and put her on display to the public. This was a major departure from tradition, as Royal Yachts were traditionally scuttled, or broken up following decommissioning. At the time, it was also a relatively high risk approach given the sensitivities associated with *Britannia's* historical role, and concerns over whether a non-Navy organisation could properly look after the former Royal Yacht.

Whilst organisations were invited to bid to become the new owners, the purchase price was pre-set at £250,000 to all interested parties. The bids were judged on their quality, appropriateness and how each would ensure that *Britannia* was maintained in keeping with her former role. Seven bids were initially considered: Glasgow, Edinburgh, Manchester, Portsmouth, and three from London. Ultimately, the Edinburgh and Manchester bids were shortlisted for more detailed consideration, with Edinburgh succeeding. *Britannia* arrived in Edinburgh on 5 July 1998, the same day that Bob Downie was appointed as the first Chief Executive of The Royal Yacht *Britannia* Trust. It was his responsibility to create the vision for The Royal Yacht *Britannia's* new life in Edinburgh.

Britannia and *Bloodhound*

Britannia's Visitor Centre, in Ocean Terminal, features many artefacts from her time in service

Great care is taken to ensure *Britannia* still upholds royal standards

Five-star visitor attraction and events venue

The Royal Yacht *Britannia* Trust opened *Britannia* to the public in October 1998. In the first year, *Britannia* attracted over 400,000 visitors, twice as many as originally expected. Now *Britannia* attracts approximately 300,000 visitors annually and has consistently been judged 'Scotland's best visitor attraction' by the national tourism agency, VisitScotland.

When *Britannia* moved to her final berth next to Ocean Terminal shopping centre in 2001, much of the Main Deck was opened to the public, showing more of the Yachtsmen's Quarters and working side of the ship in contrast to the Royal Apartments. The audio handset tour covers five decks, with highlights including the Royal Bedrooms, State Dining Room and Engine Room. The majority of items visitors see are original to the Yacht and on loan from The Royal Collection, Ministry of Defence and the *Britannia* Wardroom Officers' Trust. The Royal Deck Tea Room and Gift Shop further add to the experience for visitors.

In addition to being a popular visitor attraction, *Britannia* is now one of the UK's top venues for evening hospitality. By treating guests to a truly unique and memorable experience, *Britannia* continues to keep the spirit of Royal occasions alive. Exclusive dinners and receptions are held onboard, with exquisite cuisine freshly prepared in the Royal Galleys. On average, *Britannia* hosts 80 such events a year.

The Trust

The Royal Yacht *Britannia* Trust's overriding charitable objective is 'to advance the education of the general public concerning The Royal Yacht *Britannia*, a vessel of historical significance, and to foster, improve, promote, and increase public knowledge, understanding and appreciation of The Royal Yacht *Britannia*.'

In doing so the Trust strives to 'promote the permanent and dignified preservation, maintenance and use of The Royal Yacht *Britannia*, in a manner consistent with her dignity as a former Royal Palace.'

A self-funded, not-for-profit charitable organisation, The Royal Yacht *Britannia* Trust owns and preserves *Britannia* for future generations to enjoy. The Trust's first Chairman was Viscount Younger of Leckie KT KCVO TD DL (former Secretary of State for Defence), fondly known to one and all as George Younger. He was succeeded by Rear Admiral Neil Rankin CB CBE who took over the post in January 2003.

All surplus funds from admissions, events, the Royal Deck Tea Room and Gift Shop go back into preserving *Britannia*. There are no longer 220 Royal Yachtsmen devoted to her upkeep and wellbeing. However, today a dedicated team of 18 expert staff, led by a Naval Architect, ensures she is maintained to the highest standards. Most of this in-house team have either a Royal Navy or Naval Dockyard background. In addition to the maintenance team is a housekeeping team of 7, who keep the public areas spotlessly clean. Marine surveyors carry out an independent survey of all areas above and below deck every year. The Yacht's hull is also inspected annually by qualified divers. *Britannia* last went into dry dock in January 2012 and it is estimated this will take place every 20 years or so, when her hull below the water line will be power washed and repainted.

Britannia is also now a member of the Core Collection of the National Register of Historic Vessels, the official register of the most important British ships still in existence.

A dedicated maintenance team keep *Britannia* in 'ship shape'

Gold Leaf is delicately painted onto the Binnacle

'Dixie' and 'Norrie' raise the flag, 2013

Association of Royal Yachtsmen

Britannia is proud to be the official headquarters of the Association of Royal Yachtsmen, or 'Yotties,' who visit each year to work onboard alongside the Yacht's current maintenance team during 'Yotties Week'. The Association was founded in 1989 by Albert 'Dixie' Deane MBE RVM and is dedicated to bringing together as many of the estimated 2,400 'Yotties' who served aboard *HMY Britannia*. The Queen is Patron of the Association and the Duke of Edinburgh the President.

A bronze statue stands at *Britannia*, commissioned by the Trust, as a tribute to the Officers and Royal Yachtsmen who served onboard. The statue model was Ellis 'Norrie' Norrell MVO RVM *Britannia's* longest serving Royal Yachtsman who served 34 years, from January 1954 to September 1988.

In 2013, as part of the 60th Anniversary celebrations to mark the launch of *Britannia*, a new flag was specially commissioned in honour of all those who served aboard *Britannia*. On 16 April at 2:15pm, the same time *Britannia* was launched from John Brown's Shipyard in Clydebank in 1953, the flag was raised by 'Norrie' and 'Dixie', the two longest serving former Royal Yachtsmen.

Britannia returning from dry dock, 2012

Dry docking

I n January 2012, in a historic operation many years in the planning, The Royal Yacht *Britannia* was moved from her berth in Leith to a neighbouring dry dock for inspection and repainting of her hull below the waterline.

Britannia was last in dry dock in May 1998 when she first arrived in Leith. Whilst *Britannia* spent only fourteen days in the Leith dry-dock, to ensure that this iconic vessel was looking her best for The Queen's Diamond Jubilee year, the attraction closed for the full month. *Britannia's* maintenance team took this opportunity to repaint the masts and funnel, as well as do many other jobs on the tour route that could only be completed whilst closed to the public.

Britannia being tugged into dry dock, 2012

Insurance surveyors gave *Britannia's* hull a clean bill of health and it is thought it will be another twenty years before she has to go back into dry dock again. This is a great testament to the work that was undertaken when *Britannia* first arrived in Leith in May 1998, and to the original builders at John Brown's Shipyard, Clydebank.

And so, after a short break, over 2,500 litres of paint and hundreds of man hours The Royal Yacht *Britannia* returned to her permanent berth and reopened to the public on 1 February 2012, in excellent shape for The Queen's Diamond Jubilee Year - one of the busiest and most exciting seasons in recent years.

Britannia in dry dock, 2012

Royal Racing
Yacht *Bloodhound*

Bloodhound sailing on open water

Prince Charles sailing *Bloodhound*, 1965

DISTINCTIONS	DATES
Morgan Cup ~ Winner	1936
Channel Race ~ Winner	1936, 1939, 1951, 1958
Fastnet Race ~ Winner	1939, 1949
Cowes Week ~ Series of 1" places	1946 onwards
Southsea - Brixham Race ~ Winner	1947
Portsmouth - Poole Race ~ Winner	1949
North Sea Race ~ Winner	1949, 1951
St Malo - Dinard Race ~ Winner	1951
Harwich - Hook Race ~ Winner	1951
Lyme Bay Race ~ Winner	1959, 1965

The classic 1930s ocean-racing yacht *Bloodhound* was owned by Her Majesty The Queen and Prince Philip in the 1960s and aboard which both Prince Charles and Princess Anne learned to sail.

Members of the Royal Family, and particularly Prince Philip, have always been keen sailors. Prince Philip owned *Coweslip*, designed and built by the legendary Uffa Fox, and was given the International Dragon Class *Bluebottle* as a wedding gift. *Bluebottle*, skippered by the Sailing Master Lieutenant Commander Graham Mann, was part of the British Olympic team for the 1956 Melbourne Games and won a bronze medal. In fact, *Britannia's* hull colour was taken from this very same racing yacht. However, as the Royal children grew older, Prince Philip wanted a larger yacht with sleeping accommodation, which could undertake family cruises.

Built in 1936 by the famous Camper & Nicholson's yard in Gosport, *Bloodhound* was one of the most successful ocean-racing yachts ever built, winning scores of races in the south of England and also crossed the Atlantic to compete in Bermuda.

On the back of this outstanding race history, *Bloodhound* was acquired by the Royal Family in 1962 and Prince Philip had much success competing with her at the famous Cowes Week Regatta around the Isle of Wight. During this sailing festival *Britannia* hosted not only the British Royal Family, but members of other Royal Families and many dignitaries.

Bloodhound sailing in the Western Isles, 2012

During Royal ownership *Bloodhound* would also accompany *Britannia* in the Western Isles when the Royal Family had their one true family holiday every year. She had a permanent crew of three and one Skipper was a descendent of Sir Francis Drake. It was during these happy times that the young Royals learned to sail on *Bloodhound*. When not in Royal use, *Bloodhound* and her crew were made available to yacht clubs across the country and used to teach thousands of young people how to sail.

In 1969 *Bloodhound* was sold and not replaced by the Royal Family. *Bloodhound* then effectively retired from racing. Over time she gradually fell into considerable disrepair and very nearly became beyond salvage. However in 2003 she was purchased by Tony McGrail, a yacht surveyor and classic yacht restorer. Over the next three and a half years she underwent a major internal and external refit to bring her back to her original pristine condition.

Today *Bloodhound* is crewed by former Yachtsmen, 2011

Bloodhound was purchased by The Royal Yacht *Britannia* Trust in January 2010 and further modifications were made to improve her internal accommodation in 2013. Each year during July and August, *Bloodhound* sails to Oban where she is available for day charter around the Western Isles, crewed mainly by former Royal Yachtsmen from *Britannia*. In 2011, her maiden season back on the West Coast, Princess Anne and Admiral Laurence sailed *Bloodhound*; rekindling teenage memories of celebrating her birthday onboard. Throughout the rest of the year she is usually on display alongside *Britannia* as part of the Royal Sailing Exhibition created upon her arrival.

Bloodhound by the Forth Bridges, 2011

Maintaining Royal Connections

A bagpiper at the top of the Royal Brow

Wedding Celebrations

On 29 July 2011, *Britannia* was the venue for Zara Phillips and Mike Tindall's pre-wedding drinks reception, attended by over 140 guests. It was a truly special event for the *Britannia* team to organise and the Trust was delighted to welcome many Royal guests back onboard for the first time since decommissioning.

Zara Phillips and Mike Tindall at their pre-wedding drinks reception aboard *Britannia*, 2011

Members of the Royal Family disembark *Britannia*, 2011

15 years on, *Britannia's* Royal Barge once again carries The Queen and Prince Phillip, Thames Diamond Jubilee Pageant 2012

Britannia's Royal Barge and two Fast Motor Launches crewed by former Royal Yachtsmen during the Diamond Jubilee Pageant

The newly commissioned royal rowing barge, *Gloriana* led the man powered boats during the Pageant

HM The Queen's Diamond Jubilee

In 2012, the Trust was honoured that *Britannia's* Royal Barge and Escort Boats were invited to play a historic ceremonial role in Her Majesty's Thames Diamond Jubilee Pageant on 3 June. For the first time in over 15 years, The Queen and The Duke of Edinburgh, accompanied by The Prince of Wales and The Duchess of Cornwall, started their Pageant journey by stepping aboard the Royal Barge they once used so often around the world. The Royal Barge was escorted by both of *Britannia's* Fast Motor Launches (Escort Boats), with all three boats crewed by former Royal Yachtsmen.

After 14 years on display, *Britannia's* maintenance team, working with former Royal Yachtsmen, were tasked with making all three boats seaworthy again. Each boat was lifted on a cradle to undergo electrical, mechanical and aesthetic work, ensuring they were in immaculate condition for their Royal guests. The biggest challenge was bringing the engines back to life after having lain idle for 14 years; a heroic task for which 'Yottie' Brian Todhunter was subsequently awarded the Royal Victorian Medal (RVM).

The final stage of preparations took place during "*Britannia's* Yotties' Week", as all three boats underwent successful sea trials. After a few final finishing touches, the boats were ready to be transported in a lorry convoy down to London for the pageant.

Following the appearance at the Pageant, the Royal Barge had a wonderful welcome home as visitors lined *Britannia's* decks, waving and cheering as she was craned back into position.

Britannia's
Deck Plans

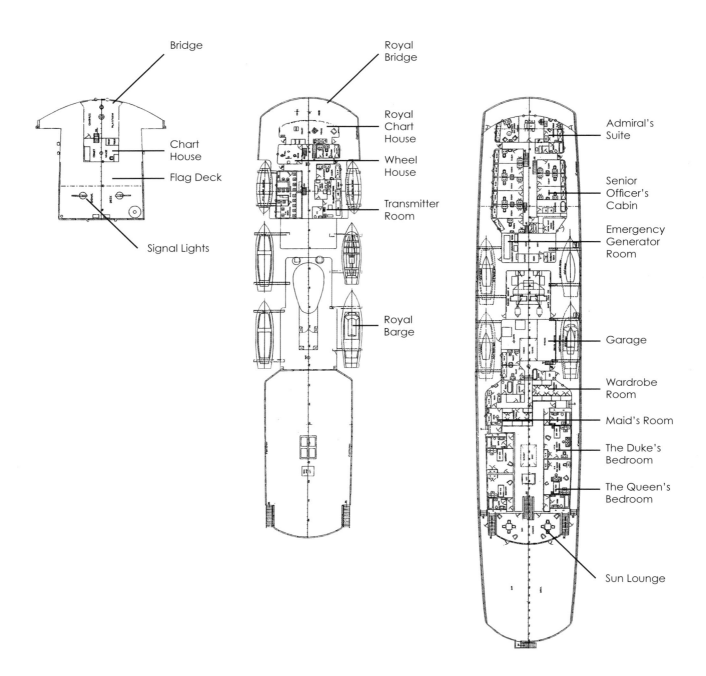

Bridge

Chart House

Flag Deck

Signal Lights

Royal Bridge

Royal Chart House

Wheel House

Transmitter Room

Royal Barge

Admiral's Suite

Senior Officer's Cabin

Emergency Generator Room

Garage

Wardrobe Room

Maid's Room

The Duke's Bedroom

The Queen's Bedroom

Sun Lounge

Compass
Platform

Bridge Deck

Shelter Deck

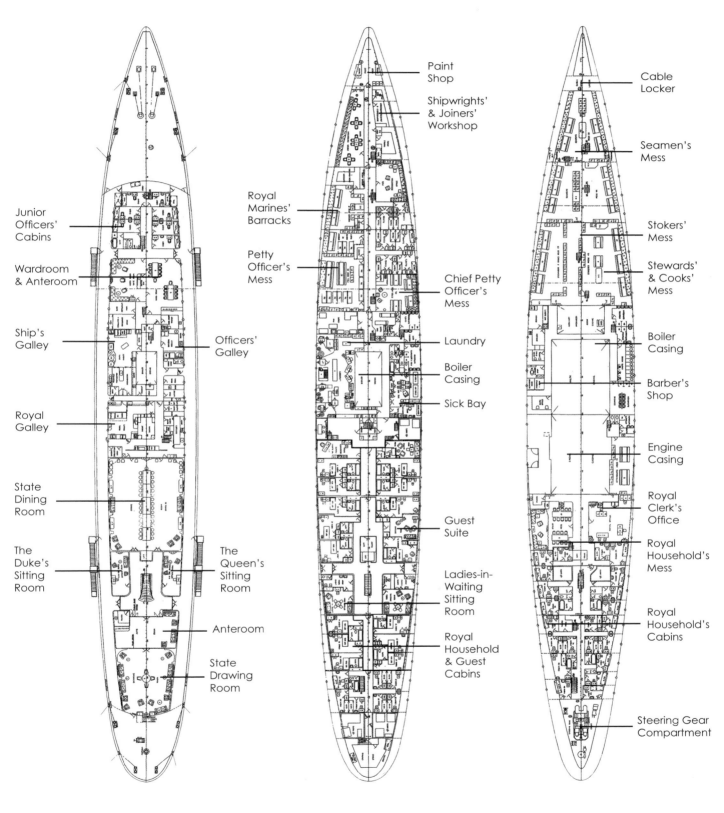

Junior Officers' Cabins

Wardroom & Anteroom

Ship's Galley

Officers' Galley

Royal Galley

State Dining Room

The Duke's Sitting Room

The Queen's Sitting Room

Anteroom

State Drawing Room

Paint Shop

Shipwrights' & Joiners' Workshop

Royal Marines' Barracks

Petty Officer's Mess

Chief Petty Officer's Mess

Laundry

Boiler Casing

Sick Bay

Guest Suite

Ladies-in-Waiting Sitting Room

Royal Household & Guest Cabins

Cable Locker

Seamen's Mess

Stokers' Mess

Stewards' & Cooks' Mess

Boiler Casing

Barber's Shop

Engine Casing

Royal Clerk's Office

Royal Household's Mess

Royal Household's Cabins

Steering Gear Compartment

Upper Deck

Main Deck

Lower Deck

Britannia Dossier

Laid down:
June 1952 at John Brown & Co. Ltd, Clydebank

Designer/Builder:
Sir Victor Shepheard, Director of Naval Construction;
and John Brown & Co. Ltd

Launched:
16th April 1953 by HM Queen Elizabeth II

Commissioned:
At sea, 11th January 1954

Length overall:
125.65m or 412ft 3in

Length on waterline:
115.82m or 380ft

Length between perpendiculars:
109.73m or 360ft

Maximum breadth moulded:
16.76m or 55ft

Breadths at upper deck moulded:
16.61m or 54ft 6in

Depth moulded to upper deck 45ft abaft midships:
9.90m or 32ft 6in

Depth moulded to upper deck at fore perpendicular:
12.29m or 40ft 4in

Depth moulded to upper deck at after perpendicular:
10.31m or 33ft 10in

Load displacement:
4,715 tons

Mean draft at load displacement:
5.2m or 15ft 7in

Gross tonnage:
5,862 tons

Shaft horsepower:
12,000

Mainmast Height:
42.44m or 139ft 3in - Royal Standard

Foremast Height:
40.54m or 133ft - Lord Admiral's Flag

Mizzenmast:
36.22m or 118ft 10in – Union flag

Fuel & Water:
330 tons of fuel oil providing a range of 2,000 miles
at 20 knots 120 tons of fresh water. Additional tanks
can increase fuel capacity to 490 tons and fresh
water capacity to 195 tons

Propeller Diameter:
3.12m or 10ft 3in

Pitch:
2.74m or 9ft

Developed blade area:
5.17m^{2}or 55.7ft^2

Tip clearance from hull:
0.84m or 2ft 9in

Maximum rudder torque:
125 tons ft at 14 knots astern and 30.5° angle

Rudder torque at 22 knots:
69 tons ft at 35° angle

Rudder torque at 15 knots:
33 tons ft at 35° angle

Maximum normal rudder force:
63.5 tons at 22 knots ahead, and 25.5 tons at 14 knots
astern

Speed:
22.5 knots maximum, 21 knots continuous

Engines:
Two geared steam turbines, developing a total of 12,000
shaft horsepower. Two main boilers and an auxiliary boiler
for harbour requirements, by Foster Wheeler

Range:
2,196 miles at 20 knots (burning diesel fuel)
2,553 miles at 18 knots (burning diesel fuel)

Acknowledgements

Illustration by John Marshall: p.10 & 11

Illustrations by Jim Proudfoot: p.46 & 47

© Sir Hugh Casson Ltd. By kind permission of Carola Zogolovitch from original watercolour
drawings by Hugh Casson RA:
p.7 (top, middle & bottom)

© UK Crown Copyright/MOD. Reproduced with the permission of the Controller of Her
Majesty's Stationery Office:
p.17 (middle), p.23 (top left), p.24 (middle left), p.25 (middle right), p.35 (top),
p.43 (bottom), p.44 (bottom), p.49, p.51 (top), p.52 (top), p.53 (bottom), p.56,
p.57 (top & bottom), p.63 (bottom)

© Press Association Images:
Front cover, p.2, p.4, p.24 (middle right), p.25 (top, middle left & bottom left),
p.34 (middle), p.40 (bottom), p.50 (top & middle), p.51 (bottom), p.52 (bottom),
p.53 (top), p.55 (bottom), p.58 (bottom), p.59 (bottom), p.60, p.61 (bottom left & right),
p.62 (top & bottom), p.72 (bottom right), Back cover

© UK Crown Copyright, IWM:
p.23 (top right), p.26, p.36, p.42 (top), p.44 (top), p.48 (top & bottom), p.55 (top), p.58 (top), p.59
(top), p.61(top & middle), p.63 (top)

© Imperial War Museum: p.45, p.54

Getty Images:
p.12, p.24 (top left, top right & bottom left), p.28 (bottom)

Royal Collection Trust/ © Her Majesty Queen Elizabeth II 2013:
p.24(bottom right), p.25 (bottom right), p.72 (bottom left)

Photograph by Yousuf Karsh/Camera Press London: p.5 (middle right)

RIBA Library Photographs Collection: p.6 (bottom)

National Maritime Museum, Greenwich, London: p.8 (top & middle)

Photograph by Helen Pugh: p.23 (middle top)

Photograph by Andrew Kavanagh: p.67 (top)

Onboard photographs by Eric Thorburn:
p.13, p.15 (top left & right), p.17 (bottom), p.20 (top & bottom),
p.21 (top left & right, middle top & middle bottom), p.27 (top & middle), p.29 (top left),
p.30 (top & middle), p.31(top & bottom), p.41 (middle)

The Daily Telegraph: p.70 (middle)

Carl Sims, Rex Features: p.43 (top)

Beken of Cowes: p.70 (top)

Reuters/Andrew Winning: p.73 (top)

ECP/Andy Rain: p.73 (bottom)

Capture the Event: p.73 (middle)

Photographs by Marc Miller:
p.14 (top), p.16 (top, middle & bottom), p.18 (bottom), p.20 (middle),
p.22 (top, middle & bottom), p.23 (middle bottom & bottom), p.29 (bottom), p.32 (bottom),
p.35 (bottom), p.39 (top, middle top & middle bottom), p.40 (top left, top right & middle),
p.41 (top), p.62 (middle)

Photographs by Ruth Armstrong:
p.15 (bottom), p.17 (8 artefact images top), p.18 (top & middle),
p.19 (top, middle & bottom), p.21 (bottom), p.28 (top), p.32 (top & middle),
p.33 (top & bottom), p.34 (top & bottom), p.37 (top, middle left & middle right),
p.38 (middle left, middle right & bottom), p.39 (bottom), p.41 (bottom right),
p.68 (middle & bottom), p.69 (bottom), p.71 (top)

Photographs by Tony Marsh:
p.67 (bottom), p.68 (top), p.69 (top & middle), p.71 (middle & bottom), Inside back cover

© Andy Gray Digital: p.66

Shannon Tofts: p.72 (top)